HOW TO RUN AN ONLINE BUSINESS

26 best tips and tricks to help you run and market

a successful online business

Written by Sephora Black

Copyright © Sephora Black, 2015

All rights reserved.

Except for use in review, any reproduction or utilization of this book in whole or in part, in any form by any electronic, mechanical, or other means, now known or hereafter invented, is forbidden without the permission of the author.

All characters and events in this book are fictive. Any resemblance to actual persons, living or dead, or to actual events is purely coincidental.

TABLE OF CONTENTS:

Disclaimer:

HOW TO RUN AN ONLINE BUSINESS

INTRODUCTION

1. FIND A NICHE

2. SELL WHAT SELLS, NOT WHAT YOU LIKE

3. USE SEARCH ENGINES

4. PRODUCT DESCRIPTION

5. HIGHLIGHT THE BENEFITS OF YOUR PRODUCT

6. INSPIRE YOUR BUYERS

7. WRITE A BUSINESS PLAN

8. NAME YOUR BUSINESS AND MAKE IT LEGAL

9. WATCH TRENDS

10. BUILD A SUBSCRIBER BASE

11. BUILD A BRAND

12. GIFTS

13. FREE SHIPPING

14. TELL YOUR STORY

15. UPDATE YOUR WEB SITE

16. HAVE A GREAT IMAGES ON YOUR WEB SITE

17. MAKE A LOGO

18. SOCIAL LINKS

19. WE DO WHAT OTHER PEOPLE DO

20. MAKE A SALE OR A DISCOUNT

21. SOCIAL PROOF

22. CUSTOMER REVIEWS

23. WATCH YOUR COMPETITION

24. READ AND FOLLOW

25. FOCUS

26. PACKING YOUR PRODUCT

AT THE END

Disclaimer:

The information contained in this book is for general information purposes only. The statements contained herein have not been evaluated nor approved. This book is sold with the understanding the author and/or publisher is not giving medical advice, nor should the information contained in this book replace medical advice, nor it is intended to diagnose or treat any disease, illness or other medical condition.

While we endeavor to keep the information up to date and correct, we make no representations or warranties of any kind, express or implied, about the completeness, accuracy, reliability, suitability or availability with respect to the book or the information, products, services, or related graphics contained book for any purpose. Any reliance you place on such information is therefore strictly at your own risk.

HOW TO RUN AN ONLINE BUSINESS

26 best tips and tricks to help you run and market

a successful online business

By

Sephora Black

INTRODUCTION

Hi there!

It was never a better time to start an online business than today. Even if it seems like it's too crowded for another web store, there is always a niche for you to jump in.

If you bought this book, you must have already known something about online business. Maybe you've tried starting your own business before, or you are planning your first one, and you are seeking for answers and good ideas. I will concentrate on web stores and their products, but these advices can be applicable to any kind of online businesses.

Anyone can make online business today. But there is a difference between doing it and doing it well. In this book you will get a lot of ideas, advices and explanations. And I'm trying to be clear and short.

Hope you'll enjoy it,

S. Black

1. FIND A NICHE

A niche is a specific subset of the market. So, if you want to succeed in any business, not just online, you need to find a niche. It can be a product or service you plan to provide. Also, it can be a specific market, but we will concentrate on a product or a service.

If you still don't know what you will sell, you need to do research. Here are some questions that might help you:

1. Who do you want to be your buyers? What age? How much do they earn? Which gender? What are their hobbies?
2. How will your product/service be different than other similar products/services?
3. Is there a place for you on the market? Are you going to sell locally or maybe worldwide?

When you determine who your buyers are, you need to know what they want. You can also do the research by creating a survey or talking to your friends and relatives. You may be surprised how good ideas you can get from them.

Ask them how much they would pay for the product they need. It will help you later.

Try to find a unique product or service, and you'll find a niche. Thousands of websites sell phone accessories. Do you really think there is a place for you too?

2. SELL WHAT SELLS, NOT WHAT YOU LIKE

If you ever read a writing advice that goes something like this: "write what you know" or "write what you like to read", please don't try to apply that in business.

Choosing the product you are going to sell is one of the hardest things in business. No one knows what will people want tomorrow, next week or next month. Some businessmen had a lucky guess.

So, you would like to know, but you can't. And then you concentrate on selling products you like, or product you know a lot about or you predict what will be sold. If you sell only what you like, you're limiting yourself to just one type of product.

Don't be afraid to try something new. You'll learn it. That's why you are in the business, anyway!

3. USE SEARCH ENGINES

Searching a perfect product, service or something else can be a daunting task for a new entrepreneur. But, if you know how to use them correctly, search engines can be of great help to you.

Also, you will need your products to appear high in the search engines, such as Google and Yahoo. For online business, online marketing is the most important shape of marketing. That includes not only search engines, but social networks, blogging, ads and email newsletters. But we will concentrate on directing people to your website through search engines in this chapter.

So, how to drive traffic to your website? There are two common ways and you can use both:

    1. **Search Engine Optimization (SEO)** – Basically, you have to choose the right words, content and design of your website fulfill the needs of different search engines. Some web providers offer you "SEO optimization", but choose your content carefully anyway.

    2. **Search Engine Marketing (SEM)** – It means paying a listing of your website at the top of the search results, or by the side of the results (it

depends on a search engine). It is paid advertising and words are also carefully chosen to connect an ad with your website.

You may want to hire an expert to do SEO and SEM for you. But it will help you to have a basic knowledge because you will probably add new products of your own. Pick our keywords and headings with a lot of thinking.

4. PRODUCT DESCRIPTION

You established your store and you are adding your products, so you need to write a description. It needs to be clear and concise, right? Sure. But it needs to **sell** your product, too.

Remember your target customer? When you write your product description, try to imagine him. Imagine you discuss with him. What would he ask you? And, what would you answer?

Don't hesitate to use the word "you" in your descriptions.

Use all technical information you have about a particular product. It is much better to give the facts than to say "it is a great product".

Make your description eye-catching and easy to read. Use headlines, bullet points, add space between lines and increase your font size.

Use colors. Be funny. Be simple. But, the most important – be different.

5. HIGHLIGHT THE BENEFITS OF YOUR PRODUCT

You like the features and specifications of your product, but your buyers want to hear what's in it for them. What will they get if they buy your product? That's what you need to highlight to attract more buyers.

For example, you want to sell a business book, like this one.

You may say: *It is a business book with a lot of tips and tricks for running an online business.*

Or, you can say: *It is a great business book with a lot of tips and tricks that* **will help you** *run a successful online business.*

There is a difference, right?

Determine how your product makes your buyer more happier, healthier or more satisfied, or which problem does it solve.

6. INSPIRE YOUR BUYERS

If you're selling your products online, your buyers can't actually see your products. Of course, there are pictures, and they can be really good and professional, but it's just not the same as holding a product in your hands. So, you'll need to prompt your buyers' imagination and let them feel like they *are* holding the product in their hands.

Describe how they will feel holding and owning your product. How will the product help them. Tell them about every feature your product has, don't expect them to investigate and read instructions. They won't do that.

And, most importantly, highlight the benefits of your product. (Explained in Chapter 5.)

Simplify your product/service and explain your buyers why they need to buy it. Show them what the product does in a way that they will be willing to pay for it (whatever it costs). Make them believe you offer something they want and they need.

7. WRITE A BUSINESS PLAN

Yes, I know it's expensive, and it seems like a waste of time, but you have to write a business plan. It is a strong foundation for your business and it will help you at the later stage when you'll almost certainly get lost (especially if this is your first business) and it'll help you like a map to a traveler. It is important and it will help you make decisions. Don't skip that!

Writing a business plan is an obligatory when you are seeking money for your business, but even if you don't consider writing one for yourself. If you are doing it just for yourself, it doesn't have to be difficult and you can do it, so it'll save you some money.

And, if you'll need a business plan for any purpose, you can use that one for making a formal one (as a starting point).

Make sure you include those chapters:

- **Executive Summary** – It summarizes the main things in your business plan.
- **Company Description** – It's an overview of your company, products and/or services.
- **Market Analysis** – It's what you've researched about your industry and target market.
- **Operational Plan** – These are the operations of your business, such as location, working hours, inventory... etc.
- **Organization and Management** – There you'll describe who owns the business, who manages it, who works in it... etc.
- **Product and Services** – There you'll describe products and/or services you are offering through your business.

- **Marketing and Sales** – This is where you'll explain how you plan to reach your target market and sell your products and/or services.
- **Financial Projections** – You need to predict how much your business will earn over the next five years.
- **Funding request** – Here you will define your funding needs and explain how you plan to use them, and how you plan to pay them back.

There is a lot of great resources online (like business plan tools) which can help you create your business plan.

8. NAME YOUR BUSINESS AND MAKE IT LEGAL

Maybe you already know how to name your business and/or your web store, but it might give you a headache when you'll try to choose an available domain name. It is probably already taken. So, try to think more names, as much as you can, and then check domain name availability. For online business, it is important to have short and memorable domain name.

Also, you need to be a registered business. That way you will show your buyers you are not just passing by; you are serious and you will be here tomorrow if they need you. Don't be a scam, it never lasts long.

Even if you want to buy from real wholesalers, you need to have a registered business. (Otherwise you'll just deal with resellers who claim to be wholesalers and pay more than you have to.)

You'll need to have a registered business name and tax ID. Also, you'll need a business bank account.

There are six possible business structures in the United States:

1. **Sole Proprietorship** – It is the most common and the most popular form of business; easy to start it and to manage. It is an unincorporated business

where there is no legal distinction between the company and the individual who owns it. The company doesn't need to file taxes, startup costs are very low, and you have complete control.

2. **Limited Liability Company (LLC)** – LLC is a business structure that combines the ease of a partnership with the liability protection found in corporations. Owners pay taxes directly on the LLCs profits. It may have a limited lifetime (depending on the state). It requires more effort than forming a partnership and you will probably need a lawyer's help.

3. **Partnership** – Partnerships are single businesses which have two or more owners. Each of these owners contributes to the business in some way. It requires a registration, but it's not that difficult to set it up; in most states is just filling out a form and paying a small fee. Partners share responsibility and profits.

4. **Cooperative** – Cooperatives are business created to service and benefit the owners (its customers are its owners). As you can suppose, it's not the best solution for your online business.

5. **Corporation** – It is a legal entity separate from any natural person, so its owners are free from personal liability. It means the shareholders' personal property is protected. You'll need to register a company to be considered a corporation. A corporation can sell shares to raise capital. It is more difficult and maintain corporation though. You can lose the limited liability if your records are not properly maintained.

6. **S Corporation** – It is formed through a special U.S. Internal Revenue Service (IRS) tax election and it is specifically built to avoid the double tax problem. The owners still have limited liability, but not the same extent as with a regular corporation.

9. WATCH TRENDS

If you're still picking products or you are expanding your offer, watch for online trends. Following what's trending may give you not just new ideas, but a new income.

There are several online sources which can help you watch trends, like:

- **Trend Watching** – Their insights and tools help future-focused professionals build brands that matter, products that delight and campaigns that people can't stop talking about. You can find them here: http://trendwatching.com/
- **Trend Hunter** – Trend Hunter is the world's largest, most popular collection of cutting edge ideas, fueled by insatiably curious people. Their trends, trend reports and innovation keynotes help creative people find better ideas. You can find them here: http://www.trendhunter.com/

10. BUILD A SUBSCRIBER BASE

I know – it's tough. People are overwhelmed with offers and they get dozens of newsletters in their mailboxes every day. Why should they subscribe to your newsletter, especially if you're new on the market?

Because you'll offer them something in return. A free product, a discount, or maybe an exclusive news about your new products or services.

When you get buyers to subscribe, you need to get them to like you. No. To love you. Again, you'll need to be unique and make your newsletter stand out. They need to remember you. That's the only way that will make them to come back.

11. BUILD A BRAND

Building a brand means also building an audience, but it's not the same. Building a brand means to tell your story and make customers love it. Make them remember it.

To successfully build a brand means to rise above your competitions and creating customer loyalty and recognition. It asks you to be creative and to think out of the box. Think about what's special about your business, what makes it different from the others.

Here are few steps that might help you build your brand:

1. **Create your company's look and message**
   - Think about why you started this business and what your goals are. What you came with is how you'll be seen. Your business needs to become like a real person your buyers can lean on.
   - What are you offering to your buyers? You need to determine what is specific about your product/service.
   - Think like a customer. (Or become one to do your research.) Why would you buy our product? How do you feel when you have it? Try to determine what feeling you want your buyers to have and try your best to wake that feeling with marketing and design.
   - Make a catchphrase or slogan you want your business to be connected with. It needs to be memorable and recognizable.
   - Choose a design scheme which matches your business. Incorporate it in all of your media: website, brochures, flyers, business letters, your products... etc. Basically, it means designing a logo and choosing the color scheme. Don't forget you want to be remembered, so keep it simple.

2. **Gain your customers' loyalty**

- Behind a great message, it has to stand a great product. If you don't deliver what you promise, your customers will buy elsewhere. You need to gain their trust.
- Your business needs to be transparent. Let your buyers see how you work, where you spend your money and what are your priorities.
- Research what other companies are offering and what is different in your business. You should highlight your difference – what makes your product better than the rest.
- Communicate with your buyers. Answer their questions.

3. **Promote your brand**
- Develop a marketing strategy for your brand. Apply your brand to your packaging and products, to your website and all of your marketing materials. Advertise it.
- Be present in social media. It is one of the best ways to build your brand. Post pictures, sales, discounts and other information.
- Have a great website. Everyone expects that these days. Hire a designer or use a template if you're creative and do it yourself. Tell your story.
- Be present, wherever it's possible. Try to give donations and sponsorships.

12. GIFTS

When someone gives us a great present for a birthday, we feel like we should do the same. We *need* to give something in return. It's the same with buyers (whatever you sell) – you need to give them something and they will buy your products/services.

So, how can we do that?

- **Offer a free gift with purchase.** It can bring you a second purchase.

- **Offer a content.** If you sell non-physical products, you can offer your buyers some kind of content, like free email seminars or a booklet.
- **Offer a free sample.** If you can get a product in the buyer's hands, you will probably sell it.

13. FREE SHIPPING

If there is any possibility to offer free shipping, use it. Even if that means slightly higher price of your product, it doesn't matter. It encourages buyers to buy from you, not from the competition, because they are looking for a better deal. The power is in word **FREE**.

Today everyone expects free shipping, and it's hard to stay on the market if your shipping costs are higher than your product's price. Displaying "free shipping" on your web page can be a great marketing advantage.

If you are not able to offer it, at least try to offer free shipping with a minimum order amount or minimum number of items. This should help you have more profit to cover your shipping expenses.

14. TELL YOUR STORY

You need to create a personality behind your business. A personality buyers will like. Don't be afraid to tell your story: How did you get an idea for your business? How did you start? What obstacles you needed to pass to succeed?

Ad "About Us" page on your web and fill it with interesting information about your business.

15. UPDATE YOUR WEB SITE

One of the most important things in online business is to keep your web store **fresh** and **clean**.

If you have a little luck, it will pass few months before you build your reputation. In most cases it will be years. Treat your buyers well and update your website regularly. A design is not that important as it is important to provide a great service for your buyers. Offer them a little of your personality, tell your story and approach each one of them like a real person (which they are), not just like a customer.

Make sure your store is well organized and easy to navigate. It has to be possible to do a search through your website.

16. HAVE A GREAT IMAGES ON YOUR WEB SITE

Images are important and you should pay attention to them; how they are arranged on your website and what are they saying to a customer. Not only images of your products, but also other images and even banners.

With the highest quality computers today, it comes the need to display high quality pictures. They may help you build your brand or promote and answer questions.

You will probably make your product pictures by yourself or hire a professional, but other pictures for your website must be free for use (or paid). If you can afford to buy pictures, that is great, because less people will use it. If you can't, I'll share some great royalty free pages with you:

- **Unsplash** – Free high-resolution photos, added every 10 days. You can find them here: https://unsplash.com/
- **Gratisography** – Free high-resolution pictures you can use for personal and commercial projects. New pictures are added weekly and you can find them here: http://www.gratisography.com/
- **Superfamous Studios** – You can find them here: http://superfamous.com/
- **Life Of Pix** – Free high resolution photos, no copyright restrictions. New photos added weekly. You can find them here: http://www.lifeofpix.com/
- **Startup Stock Photos** – You can find them here: http://startupstockphotos.com/
- **Pexels** – Free high-quality stock photos added daily. You can find them at: http://www.pexels.com/
- **Magdeleine** – Free high-resolution photos every day. You can find them here: http://magdeleine.co/
- **Stock Snap** – Free high-resolution photos added weekly. You can find them here: https://stocksnap.io/
- **Re: Splashed** – Free HD photos for your web and design projects. You can find them here: http://www.resplashed.com/
- **Picography** – Free high-resolution photos you can find here: http://picography.co/
- **ISO Republic** – High-quality free photos. You can find them here: http://isorepublic.com/
- **Stokpic** – Free photos for personal and commercial use. You can find them here: http://stokpic.com/
- **Refe** – Royalty free, high-quality, natural looking photos. You can find them here: https://getrefe.com/
- **SplitShire** – Free pictures you can find here: http://www.splitshire.com/

And also some great free editors, to help you adjust your pictures:

- **Pixlr** - A web-based or downloadable editor which is pretty easy to understand if you know the basics of editing. You can find it here: https://pixlr.com/
- **PicMonkey** - It is web-based editor, very simple for beginners. You can find it here: http://www.picmonkey.com/
- **Gimp** - It's free and downloadable software for photo retouching, image composition and image authoring. You can find it here: http://www.gimp.org/

17. MAKE A LOGO

I think logo is still underestimated. It is a recognizable sign of your business, it promotes your brand, and you should really try doing it right!

You can hire a designer or you can design a logo by yourself, using logo generator.

Here are some tips to make a great logo:

- Use one or two colors.
- Make it simple. Customers must recognize it easily.
- Make sure it looks good at smaller sizes.
- Make it memorable.
- Make sure it looks good in black & white.

Here are some free logo generators:

- **Hipster Logo Generator** - It is easy generator, filled with tools. You can find it here: http://www.hipsterlogogenerator.com/
- **GraphicSprings** - It is free to design logos, and if you're satisfied you have to pay 39,99$ to download it. But it has great features and you should seriously consider it. You can find it here: https://www.graphicsprings.com/

18. SOCIAL LINKS

Today, it is not possible to run a business without a social media presence.

The basics are to be present on Twitter, Facebook, Google+, LinkedIn, Pinterest and Instagram. When you build a website, add those cute little social buttons everywhere. People will more likely buy something others recommend. Be sure to let them share, comment and rate your products.

Choose only networks you will be able to properly manage because there is no point in making a profile somewhere if you won't be present there.

Set up your profiles and upload photos that will describe your business best. After that, build a following and start connecting with people. It will be hard from the beginning, but if you dedicate some time to it every day, soon you'll have your first 100 followers and everything after that will be easier.

19. WE DO WHAT OTHER PEOPLE DO

Because we are social beings. And we can't escape that, no matter how hard we tried.

So, if you want your buyers to copy a behavior which will make you profit, you should try these tips:

1. **Credentials** – If you can manage to get some famous or professional person talk about your product, that is a great trigger.
2. **Quote** – If you receive good comments or reviews from your buyers, make sure to quote them.
3. **Popularity of your product** – Make a "most popular" or "best-selling" page on your website.

20. MAKE A SALE OR A DISCOUNT

There are many tactics to make your buyers think they will miss their chance if they don't buy your product right now. My favorite is a countdown sale (I put a countdown clock on my website) and "out of stock" sale – when you announce a small amount of your product left.

You can also limit one of your products or make it available for just a certain time.

21. SOCIAL PROOF

At online business it may seem hard to prove you are doing well and selling your product because it is not visible to other buyers (like when you come to a real shop and see people there). So, you need to show it:

- by showing how many visits you have on your website,
- how many sold products you have or
- by social following.

It is great to mention how many satisfied customers you have and put their testimonials and/or reviews.

22. CUSTOMER REVIEWS

Many entrepreneurs still don't realize the importance of customer reviews. I didn't, either. Until I read how customers are more likely to buy your product if it has more than fifty reviews. Fifty reviews! How on earth should I get that?!

Well, first, we need to make sure to have review app on our website.

You can also arrange that buyers get an email after purchase, asking them to review the product.

And, if you can get a celebrity review, that's great! Contact them, you have nothing to lose.

23. WATCH YOUR COMPETITION

Not in a bad way though. While you check them out, try to learn something and improve your business. Don't stay behind them.

You probably already know who your competitors are, but try to find them more online. Search them and watch the ones that will pop out at the top.

Here are some important things to watch:

- How does their website look like? Is it easy to navigate? Are they up to date?
- How many products do they offer? How the pictures and descriptions look like?
- What is the price of their product? What about shipping?
- What kind of customer support do they have?
- What social accounts are they present on? How often? What do they post?

24. READ AND FOLLOW

Product review sites and blogs can be a great source of tips, ideas and inspiration.

Here are some popular places:

- **Uncrate** – http://uncrate.com/
- **Outblush** – http://www.outblush.com/
- **Bless This Stuff** – http://www.blessthisstuff.com/
- **Cool Material** – http://coolmaterial.com/
- **Gear Moose** – http://gearmoose.com/
- **Werd** – http://www.werd.com/
- **HiConsumption** – http://hiconsumption.com/
- **Firebox** – http://www.firebox.com/

25. FOCUS

When starting a new business, you may become distracted. It is normal, and it happens all the time. You may feel overwhelmed and you have too many obligations, but it is important to keep focus. If you don't get yourself together at the right time, your business can fail.

A lack of focus mostly means wasting your time. And time is money, right?

At first, start with a smaller range of products. You can expand your offer later when you get familiar with your business.

If you lost your focus in marketing, concentrate on just one channel. E.g. Run Facebook ads and spend your time gathering likes (or friends) and post there. When you accomplish your goals, go to another channel.

Prioritize your tasks. What is urgent and what can wait? Is there something you can skip?

There are plenty of apps that can make you be more productive. Here is one I like:

- **Rescue Time** – It tracks time spent on applications and web sites, giving you an accurate picture of your day. You can find it here: https://www.rescuetime.com/

26. PACKING YOUR PRODUCT

Not so far in the past, when we received a product bought online, we didn't expect anything else than just receiving the product we bought online. Today it's a bit different.

I wrote before about free shipping, so I will not repeat it here, except mentioning that we expect everybody to offer free shipping today. The other thing is, we expect our package to be a part of the product presentation. So, how will an entrepreneur achieve that?

Don't underestimate small details like a thank you note or a better quality paper your product is wrapped in.

Consider Uline products (you can find them at http://www.uline.ca/) for your packaging. Or you can search any other online, there is a variety of suppliers.

AT THE END

Thank you for reading *How To Run An Online Business*. I hope you enjoyed it.

If you would like to be notified of new book releases, please visit my web page and sign up.

Thank you!

http://bit.ly/1GSsZ0b

You can contact me through my social accounts:

Google+: https://plus.google.com/u/0/113752225373273746179/posts/p/pub

Facebook: https://facebook.com/sephorablackauthor

Twitter: https://twitter.com/SephoraBlack

LinkedIn: https://hr.linkedin.com/pub/sephora-black/b8/a90/745

Pinterest: https://www.pinterest.com/sephorablack/

Or my email:

sephora.black.contact@gmail.com

www.ingramcontent.com/pod-product-compliance
Lightning Source LLC
Chambersburg PA
CBHW021000180526
45163CB00006B/2434